THE HERO'S VOICE

Finding the Courage to Speak Out

MIKE FAIRCLOUGH

Portraits by Monica Felgendreher

Fisher King Publishing

THE HERO'S VOICE

Published worldwide by Fisher King Publishing
fisherkingpublishing.co.uk

Cover design by Tali Digirolamo

To my beautiful and powerful wife, Sundeep Sitara. Thank you for your fearless love, your strength in the face of adversity, and for your unwavering inspiration on this journey.

Novak Djokovic. Serbian world number one tennis player. He did not allow governments to blackmail him into undergoing a compulsory Covid-19 vaccination in 2022. He made clear that he believes in personal freedom of choice and supports an individual's right to choose whether or not they receive a vaccine.

Contents

Roger Waters. Lead singer of Pink Floyd. Political activist.

About the Author

Mike Fairclough is an internationally acclaimed educator with thirty years' experience in the field, the past twenty of which he has been a high-profile headteacher. Throughout this time, he has been at the forefront of character education and has created an approach to self-development which includes risk-taking, the concept of moving people out of their comfort zones and the building of resilience. His three published books, *Playing With Fire, Wild Thing and Rewilding Childhood* have been dedicated to the empowerment of adults and children alike. He has received widespread UK and international mainstream media coverage for his work. During the Covid-19 pandemic, Fairclough was the only UK headteacher or school principal to publicly speak out about lockdowns, masking and the Covid vaccine rollout to children. It is the silence from his education colleagues on this matter, as well as the growing phenomenon of people self-censoring about other urgent topics, which has prompted him to write *The Hero's Voice*.

About the Artist

Monica Felgendreher is a German activist and artist. She was one of the key leaders of the anti-lockdown movement in Berlin, after which she turned her art towards challenging government overreach and empowering others to speak out. Born in Montreal, she studied painting at the Academy of Fine Arts in Munich under the tutelage of the renowned artist, Nikolaus Lang. She travels the world exhibiting her *Performance for Peace* portraits in public spaces. A selection of these portraits illustrate *The Hero's Voice*.

Edward Snowden. Whistleblower.

Foreword

Tall, long-hair, open collar shirt, bell bottoms, sitting atop an Arctic Cat ATV is the image cast by modern day British Hero and schoolmaster, Mike Fairclough. His trailblazing efforts in education feature 'risk-taking' and the development of courageous, independent, critical thinking by his pupils. He came in popular orbit during the pandemic as an advocate for civil liberties and protectorate of children who were offered up as innocent lambs to the unsafe, ineffective, mass indiscriminate Covid-19 vaccine campaign.

Fairclough's story is one that needs to be told. This beautifully illustrated book is well-written and punchy. It drives home the fundamental message that free speech is the steel girder framework for which all civil liberties are crafted and defended. Fairclough with The Hero's Voice - Finding the Courage to Speak Out stands today with his book as a sentinel, or an early warning system, for what has become a world-wide, contagious groupthink causing the human mind to grow dark. To be pitted against family, friends and government in an epic struggle for rationalism, freedom and the pursuit of inalienable rights. Sit back and enjoy this fast-moving account of what happened to this English schoolmaster. Learn how he responded with moral courage against corruption, free-will versus tyranny, and how he has endured and prevailed in his fight for school-aged children. Fairclough's fight is your fight. We are blessed to have him and this book to serve as a guidepost during a time of darkness before the inevitable dawn.

Dr. Peter McCullough

Author, Courage to Face COVID-19, Preventing Hospitalization and Death while Battling the Biopharmaceutical Complex

---

Mike Fairclough's 'The Hero's Voice' is a powerful rebuttal to the growing culture of self-censorship which is rife across the world.

Free speech advocates like Fairclough and myself express our opinions lawfully and in good faith, attempting to defend our nation's hard-won freedoms and democracy. When we speak to members of the public, almost all agree with our views. When they do not, they tend to respectfully agree to disagree. It is clear that the woke mob, and their supporters within the media and political establishment, do not represent the majority. However, despite agreeing with logical and reasonable opinions, such as men not being able to give birth, anti-Semitism being abhorrent, and that children should not be subjected to untested medical treatments, few people speak out about it. This needs to change because silence only makes matters worse in the long run.

As this book suggests, the free speech path is not an easy one but the alternative, doing nothing, is worse. It is high time for everyone to stand up and speak out about the things that matter and to stop kowtowing to those who despise our freedom, democracy and the health of our nation. I hope that 'The Hero's Voice' will contribute to achieving this positive end.

Laurence Fox
British Actor and Leader of The Reclaim Party

Aya, a Berlin lockdown protester in her late 70s. Her name means "sword" and "never give up". She attended every protest throughout the pandemic and held a daily vigil outside the Berlin Chancellery for several months.
Aya died in 2022.

Introduction

*T**he Hero's Voice* empowers us to truly walk our talk with our words and through our actions in the world. To speak our truth in an age of lies. Drawing on the archetypal path of the mythological hero, this book explores means by which we may build our character and courageously voice our opinions. Particularly when our views are regarded by others as being unpopular, controversial or politically sensitive. By embracing the power of our voice, we will free ourselves from the messages and symbols of our modern age, which offer us little but tepid versions of who we ought to be. Unthinking, unquestioning and compliant, instead of enquiring and delighting in the limitless potential of our lives.

My former career in education, spanning almost thirty years, as well as my previous books, have been dedicated to the building of character. Exploring ways in which we may cultivate inner resilience and strengthen our confidence to take risks in preparation for life's challenges. Advocating that we should foster a sense of gratitude, hope and optimism to help guide us on our way. As well as recognising the enormous importance of our imagination, which I regard as our personal superpower. That often untapped creativity which we each possess but which gets dumbed down and vilified through years of schooling and ideological indoctrination. How many times have you heard that dreaming is a waste of time, curiosity killed the cat or to get your head out of the clouds? This is despite every significant creation within our rich human history having its origin in the imagination of its maker. From music, the visual arts and the sciences, through to writing and every technological advance since time immemorial. Imagination is at the root of them all. This underused asset is the key to our individual liberty and to the societal evolution of our times.

My work has also emphasised the importance of embracing change and the unknown. This is to encourage enquiry and critical thinking. Again, an increasingly maligned and cautioned against approach to existence. How dare we ask questions or venture off the beaten track. We are told it could be dangerous and that we might harm ourselves or others if we enquire beyond the boundaries of a subject. We are increasingly treated like frightened children listening to dark fairy tales about monsters and encouraged to be fearful of the unknown. Such an attitude fails to prepare us for the uncertainty and unpredictability of life. Nor does it mirror the beauty or the limitless possibilities of our unique existence.

I have dedicated my entire adult life to sharing techniques to build these character traits. Communicating my ethos through practical education, mainstream and alternative media, and in writing. I have also applied this philosophy to my own life, during times of great loss and challenge. Drawing on my inner resources has enabled me to overcome my own adversities and to learn valuable lessons from them all. Ultimately growing stronger as a result of each of the challenges which I have faced.

Sadly, we have been witnessing how these essential character traits for life are being steadily eroded by contemporary culture. Resilience is being replaced with a sense of helplessness. Enquiry and adventure replaced with fear of the unknown. Self-empowerment replaced with the outsourcing of our decision making to others. A bewildering phenomenon which is perpetuated by the mainstream media and by governments across the globe. Not only is this dangerous and corrosive for the individual, but it is also incredibly damaging to society and to humanity as a whole. A disempowered, fearful and unquestioning population is easy to control. Tyrannies, in all their forms, will take advantage of this. Whether it be an abusive partner, a micro-managing boss or a state tyranny, dictators require us to be submissive and compliant. Unable and fearful to imagine an alternative to our predicament, and certainly not to ask any questions or to express unsanctioned opinions about it.

Critical Thinking and Freedom of Speech

Over the years I have cultivated a strongly held philosophical belief in the importance of critical thinking and freedom of speech. When I encounter orthodoxies, I enjoy challenging them and then communicate my observations in speech and in writing. Always in a clear and lawful manner and with respect for other people's differing views. Educators and thinkers have adopted this approach to life for millennia. With philosophers such as Socrates advocating this method of thinking and communicating since the time of ancient Greece. However, challenging orthodoxies has become one of the greatest taboos of recent times. Critical thinking is frequently assigned to the realms of the conspiracy theorist and pointing out the obvious can become a punishable offence. Sanctions which are delivered by zealous authorities as well as by their obeying and unquestioning followers.

It was when I applied critical thinking to the subject of the Covid-19 pandemic that I discovered that tyranny had begun to take a strong foothold across contemporary society. Western populations were repeatedly instructed not to ask any questions about the measures we were commanded to follow and certainly not to express any scepticism about them. To do so could identify an individual as a potentially dangerous extremist. A threat to society and to the safety and wellbeing of others. Long-held beliefs such as the existence of natural immunity or the resilience of the majority of the population to Covid became off-limit topics of conversation. Suggesting that lockdowns would result in economic harm, and therefore damage to our health, was an enormously vilified stance to take. But the most egregious act has been to challenge the merits of the holy grail of the Pandemic; the Covid mRNA vaccines. Asking reasonable questions about these can still transform the thinker into a blasphemer and heretic of the highest order. A misdemeanour which can lead to us being criticised and punished by those in authority, as well as by our fellow citizens.

This book does not seek to persuade the reader to agree with my personal views about the global pandemic response and policies. That is not the point of it at all. Instead, it is a book which advocates the importance of speaking our truth and encourages the need for open debate. Furthermore, I hope to ignite a renewed desire for self-empowerment in the reader and to inspire a touch of rebellion. Not in a destructive or negative manner but with the intention of supporting individual self-development and our unique quests for truth. To intelligently rebel against orthodoxies and ideologies which we question or disagree with. To feel confident to stand up for what we believe in. Particularly if our beliefs and opinions are counter-narrative to the mainstream.

Throughout the Covid pandemic, I was the only headteacher or school principal in the UK (out of 20,000+) to have publicly expressed concerns about the Covid vaccines for children. My opinion is that the risks from the vaccines outweigh any possible benefits. A view which I share along with many prominent doctors, scientists, lawyers, journalists and politicians. Professionals who I have had the pleasure to campaign alongside and deliberately forged strong alliances with. I also recognise, as with all things, that other people hold opposing views to my own. However, balanced discussion about the Covid vaccines was completely shut down when they were being rolled out to children. Reasonable conversations were stifled and individuals attempting to debate on this topic were attacked. My colleagues within the education sector and many people within the wider community have remained publicly silent on this subject. Indeed, there continues to be an air of fear and caution around even the mildest debate about this controversial medical intervention.

Different opinions are a healthy and necessary feature of any democracy. Conversely, the censorship of ideas and the erosion of free speech are roads to dystopia and a profoundly undemocratic way of being. Despite this fact, expressing an alternative opinion about certain matters is increasingly regarded as anti-social and potentially dangerous in the West. This was previously the exclusive trait of authoritarian regimes, such as communist and fascist dictatorships which seek to control what their populations are allowed to say. But perhaps the most chilling aspect of this change to our society is observing how people self-censor. Watching them stay silent out of fear of reprisals if they express an unpopular opinion. No longer requiring authority figures to tell them what to think or to say but becoming their own personal censors. This is a very dangerous phenomenon and for which *The Hero's Voice* is a response. A way for us to embrace our individual beliefs and opinions and to express them courageously, despite our fears about how others may respond. After all, if we are not living and speaking our own truth, whose truth and words are we actually living?

The Hero

As a society, we urgently require symbols and role models which inspire our empowerment. Archetypes which enable us to deal with change, to face the unknown, to take risks and to become resilient. Gateways to our own, individual adventures, bringing us personal freedom, fulfilment and joy. Powerful archetypes which encourage us to have the confidence and courage to speak our truth. Particularly in the face of opposition and within climates of growing censorship. Ancient mythology and the concept of the hero's quest provides us with all of this and more. A primordial story structure which has been utilised in numerous films and books and which everyone will recognise on closer look. The image of the freedom fighter, the truth seeker and brave warrior. That person *they* do not want us to be.

> *"Our lives begin to end the day we become silent about things that matter"*
> Martin Luther King Jr

Countless mythologies and legends throughout the world share a common theme. They mirror the cycle of birth, life and death, as well as reflect the challenges we experience while alive. Within these ancient stories, the hero, or central character, often begins the tale living in relatively settled or normal surroundings. They are then called to embark on a quest, which in most cases the character at first resists. Change and transformation in the direction of adventure, and likely danger, are not welcomed. They say things along the lines of *"why choose me?"* and *"I'm not a hero"*. Preferring to carry on their lives within the safety and certainty of what they already know. The reluctant hero is strongly resistant to the quest and to what it might bring.

Eventually, the call to adventure is answered with positive action and the first stage of their journey begins. Often, this is because the alternative, doing nothing, is worse than the potential perils of the quest. Entering into unchartered territory and the unknown, the hero then embarks on their adventure. Here on in, they encounter various trials and challenges. Each one a test of the character's physical, mental, emotional and spiritual attributes. Forced out of their comfort zone and honing new or latent skills as required, the hero moves towards their goal. The thing they seek, the task they must undertake and the revelations they experience are the purpose of their journey.

Self-doubt, feelings of despair and making mistakes are typical aspects of the hero's journey. So too are moments when the character realises that they are stronger than they had previously realised. More willing to make sacrifices for others, standing up to opponents and triumphing over a range of adversities.

Towards the end of the story, the hero attains their goal. They also acquire and recognise new, often magical, inner traits. Gifts which have arisen out of their adversities. Revelations which would have remained undiscovered had it not been for the quest and its hard challenges. Finally, within most of these stories, the hero returns home. Wiser, stronger and in full knowledge of their new powers. The cycle is then complete. The main character, who to start with was resistant to the challenge of the quest, has transformed into a hero.

Tales with this format have been told across the globe for millennia. They inspire courage and strength, as well as reassure the recipient of the story that their feelings of doubt and fear are all part of the journey. Stories to guide us towards deeper truths and in the direction of our own personal quests and revelations.

Many of these myths include authority figures or cultural norms, which stifle the main character at the beginning of the story. They caution them against embarking on great quests and adventures. *"You have everything you need right here"*, *"You don't need to go beyond what you already know"*, *"Why put yourself in unnecessary danger?"*

As with the mythological hero, this familiar advice denies a person access to the powerful insights which can be gained from rising to a challenge. Those things which only the individual can attain through the lived experience of their inner and outer journeys. Our potential and life's purpose do not reside within the safety of other people's fears and limitations. Resist it or not, we are each the main character within our unique and individual stories. True tales in which we can choose to have our great adventures or our reasons for not having them.

The archetype of the mythological hero and the heroic quest are potent antidotes to an age of creeping tyranny. A powerful rebuttal to self-censorship and cultural disempowerment. This is where we can find inspiration for our empowered voice and to stand up for what we believe in. To answer the call to the quest and to become our own hero. A gift not only to ourselves but to our children and to the generations of humanity to follow.

The *Hero's Voice* is an invitation to embark on a powerful and rebellious adventure. One which will almost certainly disrupt and annoy those who would prefer us to be silent. But let us not be ruled by our fears of tyrants any longer. Voicing our personal opinions about topics which are close to our hearts is a right which we have within a free society. Silence, resulting from self-censorship and the unreasonable demands of others, must end. The time has come to pick up our swords and to speak our truth. Our call to the quest has begun.

George Orwell. Author of the prophetic and
dystopian novel 1984.

Chapter 1: The Calling

"If not us, then who?
If not now, then when?"

Martin Luther King Jr

We have all felt it. That urge to be free. To break from the chains of our limitations. Leaving behind the old ways and embracing something new, liberating and expansive.

However, in order to become free, we must first accept that we are living in a metaphorical prison. Not only that, but we must also embrace the uncomfortable truth that it is a prison of our own making. Without this realisation, no escape is possible. Instead, all that is available to us is the illusion of freedom.

Awakening to the truth of this predicament can feel incredibly empowering. Even though we are often led to this realisation by life's greatest challenges. Those seriously hard, yet enlightening times which everyone, at some point, will experience.

I have suggested that an antidote to the stifling of our free speech and self-censorship could emerge from the archetype of the mythological hero. Furthermore, the concept of the heroic journey provides an explanation as to why so many people feel resistant to speaking out. As it turns out, this is a necessary and typical part of any true quest.

The Many Roads to a Free Speech Quest

The vast majority of mythological heroes, at first, reject their call to the quest and have the same doubting feelings as our own. Do we really want our lives to be more problematic than they already are? Do we have what it takes to overcome adversity? When it comes to expressing our controversial or politically sensitive opinions, perhaps it is easier to remain silent?

There is no judgement at this point. This book is designed to inspire people's liberation, rather than provide a new and sanctimonious list of diktats for others to follow. If we are to become truly self-empowered we must embrace our own choices and free will. Giving our power and decision making to others will not serve us. This includes relinquishing our decisions to an ideology. It simply does not work if we wish to be free.

However, if we realise that the door to our prison cell is already open, we can walk right through it. The empowered option and gateway to our liberation. What adventures lie on the other side only we can discover. Ironically, this is often when we feel the least prepared and ready for a big change within our lives. Hence our resistance to it.

There are multiple ways in which we may be called to a quest of any kind and a major one is through uninvited adversity. This could be our reaction to the death of a loved one, a career ending unexpectedly, a serious health issue or a societal change which significantly impacts on us. The shock of the experience wakes us up and makes us step out into new terrain.

At other times we may intentionally alter our lives in a way which brings us great challenge, with the hope of gaining rewards. This can happen when we embark on hard physical tests. It can also be the result of any major change in our behaviour or habits. One which is very difficult but offers us potential benefits if we succeed.

A third way is when another person invites us to embark on a quest. The individual is often a mentor or inspirational figure to us. Their wisdom and example leverages us onto the next phase of our development. Numerous heroes within mythology have a mentor to guide them on their path.

We can also be called to a quest through our dreams or inspired by a spiritual vision. When we emerge from our subconscious or higher conscious state, we know exactly what we must do.

The calling may also arrive through a connection with nature. When we are standing on top of a mountain or watching a beautiful sun set into the sea. The sight fills us with awe and wonder and expands our heart and mind. These are epiphanies offered up by the elements and which can inspire our next steps.

There are also occasions when we just know that it is time. We have come to fruition within our present state of being and are now ready to grow and develop further. When we are called to the quest in this way it just happens, with no apparent external influence that we are aware of.

But what makes something a quest and not a more simplistic change in our lives? I believe it is the level of challenge it demands of us. If we are truly put to the test, venturing into unknown territory and leaving our old lives behind, we are on a real quest. We will probably feel great anxiety and trepidation before we embark on it and feel this way, at points, throughout. Our body will also tell us that we are on a new and at times perilous journey. Our gut instinct and intuition will be engaged and heightened, giving us a tingling feeling of fear and excitement. Ambiguous notions, such as hope and faith, may be our sole companions as our quest begins and will travel with us throughout our adventure.

We can also fake it and convince ourselves that we are questing. However, if we are still residing within the safety of the known, we are not on our great adventure. That visceral thing which only we can experience, be enlightened by and which reveals our inner gifts. Rewarding us with our freedom if we stay the course.

When it comes to expressing our opinions, we may fear potential conflict and attacks from others. This is one of the main reasons why so many people censor themselves. It is certainly becoming increasingly uncomfortable to publicly express unsanctioned and unpopular beliefs. But if we regard our urge to express ourselves as the call to our quest, we can prepare for this. Knowing that we will be entering a big challenge, with its various tests and victories along the way. A journey which will include our feelings of resistance but which we can overcome and be empowered by. See it through to the end and we will become stronger and wiser than we could ever have imagined. At which point, our fear of criticism will no longer shackle us to a life of public silence. We will then be confident to express our beliefs and opinions regardless of what others might say. We will have attained the hero's voice and the courage to speak out when we need to.

Governments across the world have put enormous effort into silencing and censoring the populations they lead. If they control the narrative they control the people. But when we express our opinions in the face of this opposition, regardless of the cost, we are far more difficult to control. Finding our voice gives us great personal power. We then see very clearly how weak and frightened those who try to bully us into silence truly are.

Summoning the Inner Hero

It is during our most challenging times, uninvited or not, that drawing on the archetype of the hero can be greatly beneficial. In my view, there is no better place to start than with ancient Greek mythology. One of the most extensively recorded and detailed sources of myth and incredibly rich in awe inspiring characters and stories. The famous poet, Homer, authored poetry describing the hero, Odysseus, around 2700 to 2800 years ago. The poems recount tales of Odysseus's quests which were set some five hundred years before that time, in the Greek Bronze Age. Homer is credited with creating the Iliad and the Odyssey, two epic poems which have come to be regarded as the cornerstones of ancient mythology and history. Their influence on our modern day storytelling, within film, literature and art, cannot be overstated. The poems follow the cycle of the hero's quest, as described in the introduction of this book. A story structure which is widespread across the ancient world and which chimes with the experience of our own lives today.

Odysseus is the archetypal hero, as are the female equivalents of the time, such as Atlanta. Through the lens of these characters, Homer provides us with deep insights into the human condition. Beautiful and timeless observations which have survived the ages and touch our souls to this day. The characters within these ancient tales are heroic, as well as vulnerable at times. They are fallible and make mistakes, just like we do. Homer also describes the resistance to the quest, which is regularly felt by Odysseus throughout his journey. This is a common theme shared by mythological heroes. Something which they feel before their quest has begun and at moments throughout their adventures. I believe this is why mythology is so relevant to us today. It reflects our own thoughts and feelings during times of great challenge. The example of how heroes eventually push through their resistance can motivate us when we feel this way too.

The Odyssey begins at the conclusion of the Trojan War. A long battle in which Odysseus and the Greeks were victorious. He had been away from his home and family for ten arduous years and began to long for them again. The battle was now over and he felt deeply homesick. Again, this is a typical feature within mythology. It is called "nostos" a word which is defined as the desire for homecoming. A theme within heroic myth which inspires bravery, strength and determination by reminding the hero of what they are fighting for. The desire for homecoming is what gives many of us the urge to publicly speak our truth. Not a return to a physical home but to a place of inner tranquility, peace and fulfillment. This is why, when we feel unable to freely express ourselves, we experience none of these qualities very deeply at all.

It took a further ten years for Odysseus to return to his island home of Ithaca and to his wife and son. The complete duration of his quest was twenty years. However, throughout the story, there are times when he seriously doubts his ability to achieve his goal of returning to his family. His example reminds us that it is natural to feel self-doubt and resistance when we are facing adversity. It also inspires us to draw on our inner strength, which Odysseus is forced to do on multiple occasions. Homer's retelling of the story also connects us with concepts such as love, life and loss and how we might navigate our way through them. Within our own lives, how we deal with experiences such as personal loss is where much our learning and growth comes from.

Most importantly, I believe that the main function of these stories is the deep message that we too can be heroes. Overcoming our own adversities and being victorious in life. Attaining wisdom and self-knowledge along the way. Mythology inspires us to dig deep in order to find our true strength, particularly during challenging times. It also prepares us, despite our doubts and fears, to draw our sword and step into the fray of life.

> *"To begin is the most important part of the quest and by far the most courageous"*
>
> Plato

In ancient times, mythological stories would have been told around the fire and passed down from generation to generation. Although this is still the case for some people and cultures, many of us now receive the mythic cycle and the symbol of the hero through films and books. However, the purpose of the storytelling, or at least its effect on us, is exactly the same. An ancient Greek may have left the fireside, having heard about the great quests of Odysseus, feeling inspired and emboldened. Ready for life's challenges and possibly relishing the prospect of their own adventure with eager anticipation. These days, we leave the movie theatre, having watched our cinematic heroes battle against the odds, with our own sense of determination, resilience and confidence. Feeling that we too can be strong and able to overcome our adversities.

Of course, heroes do not just exist within mythology and fictional books and films. Inspiring people, who have achieved extraordinary things from quite ordinary beginnings, are also found within physical reality. This is particularly true when it comes to free speech advocates. People who have spoken their truth in the face of adversity.

The civil rights icon, Rosa Parks, improved the lives of black people in America after taking her heroic stand against racial segregation in the 1950's. Her background and cultural circumstances were stacked against her, yet she helped change the political landscape of an entire nation in the face of enormous challenges. Malala Yousafzai, another great female hero, took on the Taliban in Pakistan and fought for girls' education. Even an attempted assassination and gunshot wound did not stop her from continuing to speak out. John Lennon, the frontman of the legendary music band "The Beatles" heralded from a tough working class background and became a world renowned musician and political campaigner. He had an ordinary start to his life, albeit a hard one, but went on to influence the world through his music and political activism. The list of historic examples could fill a library of books and of course would include the famous Martin Luther King, Ghandi and many others.

The past few years have revealed new ranks of free speech advocates and freedom fighters. The restrictive and authoritarian nature of the pandemic brought many of these people to the fore. Dr. Peter McCullough, Robert Kennedy Jr, Dr. Tess Lawrie, Sonia Elijah, Neil Oliver, Molly Kingsley and many more.

I doubt that a single person alive has not, at some point, been inspired by the heroic deeds of a fictional or real life character. Or that they have never compared the achievements of a hero to their own behaviour and then been influenced in some way. The symbol of the hero can help guide and motivate us towards our own goals and to face our challenges. Inspiring us to draw on our inner strength and to discover new qualities within us. If we go deeper, the heroic journey can also reveal further layers of reality and the spiritual dimensions of the quest. An aspect of the free speech journey which is personal to each of us and which only we can experience. This is arguably the main function of the quest.

However, the first step on our journey begins with aligning our thoughts and feelings with those of a hero. Embracing a heroic determination, courage and strength despite our self-doubt and resistance. Our metaphorical swords and shields are already at hand. They hang on the walls of our hearts and minds, along with numerous other tools and attributes yet to be discovered. So too are the rewards and prizes of the quest itself. But the hardest part, as Plato remarked, is to begin our journey. It will always be our choice as to whether or not we do so.

However, despite our feelings of resistance, the time will come when our courage eclipses our fear, if only for a moment. Just enough to cross the threshold and begin what we know we must do. We will receive great gifts and insights on our journey and there will be times when we will question our abilities. Just like every living, historical and mythological hero has experienced before us. The hero's path will light the way if we summon its energy from within. Leaving our old world behind and transforming into something new, more authentic and empowered than before. Confident to express our opinions to others and courageously speaking our truth to the world.

Robert F. Kennedy Jr. American politician, environmental lawyer, activist and Independent Candidate for President of the United States.

Chapter 2: Fear of Change and the Unknown

*"The only way to make sense of change
is to plunge into it, move with it,
and join the dance."*

Alan Watts

Why was I the only serving headteacher or school principal, out of more than 20,000 in the UK, to speak out about the Covid vaccines for children? It is not because I am brave or have any medical expertise. Nor is it the case that other headteachers did not share my concerns. I was privately thanked by many of my colleagues for taking the stance that I did but they all remained silent.

It is a legal duty of every headteacher and school principal to safeguard children against harm. It is also our moral obligation. This is why I spoke out. Nonetheless, no one else at my level within the education sector publicly raised concerns about the biggest safeguarding breach of our times. Many educators, medical professionals and other members of the public have said that they agree with me but have been too scared to speak out for fear of reprisals. This is what inspired me to write *"The Hero's Voice"*. It is essential that we empower ourselves, and others, to express our opinions. Particularly if our views are considered controversial or politically sensitive and we are self-censoring.

I regard self-censorship as being more sinister and dangerous than state censorship. Once we stop silencing ourselves, *en masse*, tyrannies and their tin-pot dictators will fall. Our silence is their power. But in order to do this, we must first conquer our fear of change and the unknown.

Embracing and Overcoming our Resistance

Resistance to change and fear of the unknown are two of the reasons why people choose not to voice their opinions about sensitive topics. Sharing our views and beliefs with the world can cause a reaction in others. This may result in negative consequences and pushback. Many of the consequences will be unknown, thus tapping into our fears about what may or may not happen to us. However, to evolve from not sharing our thoughts and opinions with others to making them public will require a degree of change.

The mythological hero is often cautioned against unwanted change and unknown danger at the beginning of their quest. *"Stick to what you know and you will be safe"*, is what they are told. This is one of the main reasons for their initial resistance to the call to adventure. Within our modern age, we too are warned about the perils of change and the unknown. Government messaging increasingly steers us in the direction of what they say is good for us. Often using fear of unwanted change and catastrophe as the main driver. Telling us that if we do not do as they advise we could put ourselves and others in mortal danger. This effective method of social control was widely used throughout the Covid pandemic.

There are multiple ways in which we are dissuaded from publicly expressing our views. When it comes to what we write and say, the public is constantly warned about the dangers of sharing "unsanctioned" opinions. Social media companies de-platform and silence us if we defy their warnings. Friends, colleagues and family members may attack or exclude us if they feel offended by our views. There is a possibility that we could be disciplined at work, lose financial opportunities or suffer reputational damage, if reported, investigated and sanctioned. It is no wonder that so many people are reluctant to express their honest opinions. They feel it is better to keep their thoughts to themselves than to risk being attacked by others. Fear of change and the unknown, as a result of exercising their right to free speech, keeps many people in silence. This is a very dangerous phenomenon and one which we cannot simply ignore. If we keep quiet about the things which matter to us, our conversational environment will recede and become increasingly smaller and tighter. It is entirely possible that we could then find ourselves in such a heavily self-censored environment that we allow unthinkable harms to take place around us. People have already demonstrated that they are willing to stand back in silence as things they fundamentally disagree with happen in front of their eyes. The hope is always that the problem will go away or that someone else will sort it out.

However, for some individuals, there is a red line. A matter so close to their heart that they have to speak out, regardless of the consequences. This has historically been the moment when many ordinary people have embarked on their heroic quest. A situation so dire and urgent that it has inspired them to feel they have no choice but to respond with action and words.

Embracing change and the unknown

We can remedy our fears by embracing change and seeing the power and potential in the unknown. Turning change into our ally and using it to our advantage. This begins by seeing change and the unknown as integral to who we are and an important element of our rich human history. As our species has evolved throughout the ages, there is abundant evidence of our relentless creativity in response to change. We can see this in the many examples of how humans have adapted to a vast range of different landscapes and climates across the globe. Changing the way in which we live, eat, work and raise our families, according to each terrain, season and historical event. On a grand scale, some of our ancestors created entire empires and later others witnessed them fall. Seemingly infinite and all powerful, each empire eventually disappeared and, in some cases, literally crumbled and turned to dust. All the time, each individual passing through the unavoidable and moving cycle of birth, life and death. No matter which person that may have been from the past and applicable to every individual alive today. Everything in life is subject to change. Our bodies, thoughts, emotions and actions in the world have a period of birth, growth, death and decay. Sometimes these phases appear to move incredibly slowly while at other times the speed at which we experience them is ferocious, instant and unexpected.

Often, change feels uncomfortable but it can also make us feel liberated and excited. More often than not, we simultaneously experience a wide range of emotions to change, as well as physical and mental reactions. The joy and excitement for something new happening is frequently accompanied by trepidation and uncertainty. We wonder whether everything will be okay as we venture into unchartered territory. The birth of a new phase will usually run parallel with the death of the old. So, again, apparently conflicting responses, such as elation and sadness, may go hand in hand.

Another, very powerful, word for change is transformation. Trans: *"across, beyond"* Form: *"a map, appearance, beauty, shape, figure"*. A movement which can travel in opposite directions or parallel in its growth and decay. When we feel that our lives are transforming into something different or new, we open ourselves to being enriched and empowered by the experience. It may also feel frightening and there will be occasions when we wish it wasn't happening at all. Transforming will flow at times and be easy but it can also be extremely challenging and difficult. Periods when a transformation puts us to the test. This is when we may try to resist and avoid change which feels uncomfortable.

Despite the discomfort, there are also moments when we consciously invite a degree of difficulty as we transform. Hoping and expecting that our efforts will bring us rewards. The phenomenon of change may look confusing, contradictory and messy but it is a constant and inevitable one. Transformation within our own lives and in the world around us is natural. Most importantly, transformation is necessary.

When we exercise our right to free speech and share what others regard as controversial opinions, we often experience intense transformation. We may find this through other people's reactions to what we are saying as well as through our own responses to speaking out. Stepping into the quest in this way will invite enormous change, some of which will inevitably feel uncomfortable.

There will also be transformation in the direction of our individual growth and expansion. We can remain in our cocoons for the rest of our lives and eventually die there if we wish to. Staying within the comfort of the known with as few avoidable problems as necessary. But that path risks missing the opportunity of being who we really are. The uncensored and liberated version of ourselves. The one which will still die in the future but with fewer regrets and resentments. An eagle on the wing having spoken our truth to the world.

"...and the Lotus-eaters did not plan death for my comrades, but gave them of the lotus to taste. And whosoever of them ate of the honey-sweet fruit of the lotus, had no longer any wish to bring back word or to return."

Homer, The Odyssey

Being open and vulnerable while also summoning our inner strength and resilience, is as powerful as it is beautiful. This is often how we feel when speaking our truth to others. Humans are not emotionless robots. We feel physical and emotional pain and our mental states can become stressed and confused during times of great challenge. But attempting to banish all feelings of discomfort and torment from our lives is unattainable, unrealistic and missing the point of our existence. Without these things we absolutely would become robotic. There is great depth and beauty within the complexity and contradictions of the human condition. Transformation and change can feel messy, raw and tumultuous. But it is how we grow and develop into our full potential.

It is also part of the human condition to attempt to resist this transformation. Change and feelings of discomfort are not always what we desire, so we often pursue safety and inertia instead. Choosing silence over speaking our truth. One of the ways in which we might attempt to avoid embarking on our free speech quest is by residing on a metaphorical *Island of the Lotus Eaters*.

The tussle between pleasure and pain is an age old battle and a feature of all heroic quests. Mythology is abundant with examples of heroes who temporarily delay the hardship of their quest in favour of physical, mental and emotional comfort. Just like us, they are seduced by physical gratification, ease and pleasure, instead of facing the hard task of their journey. Choosing not to start or continue what they know they must do.

The *Island of The Lotus Eaters* is a location which Odysseus and his crew find while on their quest. They had just escaped death on the Island of Cicones and then fled on their ships. This was followed by ten days of gigantic storms at sea, sent by the gods to destroy them and designed to end their journey. They eventually land on an island inhabited by a tribe of people who live off the fruit of the lotus tree. The fruit is highly addictive and pleasurable and creates the illusion of a personal paradise. A wonderful feeling to experience but one which removes any desire for ambition and attainment of personal goals. Ultimately erasing all memory of what was once held dear to those who consume it. Any vestige of life's purpose then slips away.

Odysseus's men fell effortlessly into this wonderful distraction and so their discomfort was eased. Many of us do this when life feels challenging. We may mask our pain with alcohol, recreational drugs, legal medication, addictive foods, caffeine or other substances. Most of these make us feel great in the moment, otherwise we would never touch them. It is also possible to enjoy many of these things without losing our way. But there is a tipping point when substances which we consume can have a corrosive effect on our wellbeing. Overreliance and excessive use of them can cause our demise. Even if we artificially maintain a continuous sense of intoxication or high with various chemicals, the feeling never lasts. There is often a far less pleasurable comedown after the experience.

Many of us also seek comfort through the trappings of convenience and modern technology. They sparkle and allure, bringing us moments of pleasure through social media, apps and gadgets. Digital technology endlessly entertains and promises to make our lives better. We are also able to get strong dopamine hits from the attention we receive online. Adrenaline rushes when our social media posts are noticed or when we follow a train of interest as we scroll through our phones. Highly addictive and highly pleasurable pursuits. Again, these are not all bad and it is entirely possible to enjoy and use these to our benefit.

However, after the hit, if the comedown feels hard, we often end up craving more. If this happens, it is a sign that we are getting trapped. This is what addictive things are designed to do. They channel our insatiable appetites to crave pleasure until we become completely reliant on them.

It is also possible to slip into pious denial of all pleasure. A Puritan approach which regards physical joy as a source of evil. This is also a trap. As physical beings we are blessed with sensuality and the ability to experience very deep happiness. However, denial of our nature and separation from our bodies can cause as much pain as addiction and excess. Again, ancient mythology is abundant with examples of the tussle with temptation and moments when the hero must reject short-term pleasure to continue their quest.

After several days, Odysseus dragged his crewmen back onto their ship. They were so deeply immersed in the bliss of intoxication that they had to be forced out of it. They were then able to continue their great adventure. Many of us too can languish within a place of complete distraction but we need to know when to leave. Like Odysseus and his men, we have our own homecoming and quests to undertake. Living and speaking our truth, without allowing this precious opportunity to slip away.

Embarking on a True Quest

A true quest must include embracing the mystery of the unknown. It requires us to take a leap of faith or at least an element of leaving behind our old and present condition. Within our quest, the unknown will almost certainly present us with a range of foes and monsters. It is not a walk in the park to voice our opinions about controversial subjects. There will also be revelations and insights. Gifts which can only emerge from the unknown and which will empower and motivate us further.

There is abundant historical evidence that our ancestors embraced change and the unknown. They ventured off the known path and explored undiscovered lands. They must also have been wary of potential attacks from hidden dangers and driven by a need to survive. But look at any mythological story and we can see that the heroes within them are not cowering away in fear. They are constantly enquiring, innovating and prepared to face the perils which confront them. In contrast, our modern age offers us safe and anesthetising alternatives to the quest. Presenting us with easy and addictive distractions. This is why I believe that the archetype of the hero and the cycle of the heroic quest is so powerful and relevant right now. Inspiring us to stand up and to speak out.

My colleagues within the education sector chose not to express their opinions about the Covid vaccines for children and other measures out of fear. I understand why they did that. It is natural not to want to make life more difficult than it already is. However, they missed a vital opportunity to safeguard children against harm. They also lost a chance to move out of their personal comfort zones and to expand.

We are approaching a time when it is likely that the authorities will say that there are new global pandemics to respond to. Children may once again be subjected to harmful measures imposed by our governments. Will those who were silent before be silent again, or will more of us answer the call to the quest next time? I believe it will be the latter. But it will require each of us to answer the call to the quest and fully embrace change and the unknown.

Frida Khalo. Mexican painter and political activist.

Chapter 3: Rebellion, Risk-Taking and Resilience

"There can't be any large scale revolution until there's a personal revolution, on an individual level. It's got to happen inside first."

Jim Morrison

I f we are going to speak out about a controversial subject and take a stand about it, we will probably stand alone. Few people are willing to publicly support those who express controversial opinions, even when they hold exactly the same beliefs in private. For the speaker, this is when rebellion, risk-taking and resilience become our closest allies. Three character traits which are often vilified and which we are frequently cautioned against. Instead of being rebellious, we are told to follow the rules. Rather than take risks, we are encouraged to choose safety. In place of being resilient, we are offered the false sanctuary of dependence and over-reliance on others.

People refrain from speaking up and speaking out because they worry about the consequences of doing so. They know that they might be cast out from their groups and even shunned by complete strangers. There is also the fear of what it might mean for their paid employment. They could lose their job or at least limit their future career prospects. Many then switch into survival and self-preservation mode. No job means no money. No money means no food or roof over their head. These are real and valid concerns.

Within ancient mythology, the hero initially resists the call to the quest for similar reasons. They have little desire to put themselves in danger or to find themselves alone in the unknown. However, when they eventually embark on the quest, to the point where it is too late to turn back, something else happens to them. They begin to dig deep within themselves and discover the strength and inner resources they need for their journey. They still feel lonely and desperate at times, but they learn to move through these uncomfortable stages, becoming stronger as they do so.

Rebellion

To make the decision to step out into the quest and invoke the hero's voice is an act of rebellion. This is because we know that other people may not want us to voice our opinions and would prefer it if we remained silent. In expressing our opinions, we may ruffle the feathers of those who rigidly believe that only their beliefs and opinions are right. In speaking up and speaking out we are rebelling against those people. It is then quite likely that they will openly attack us, as well as launch covert assaults on our right to lawful free speech. Within the workplace, this is when anonymous whistleblowing complaints are often used by those who disagree with our views. Unable to debate us face to face, they resort to underhand tactics. Often this type of person possesses a herd mentality which makes them seek out others who agree with their stance. Often forming allegiances with individuals who they previously had little or no connection with, in order to form a larger group. Speaking out about a controversial subject will be seen as a direct attack on them, so they will do whatever they can to retaliate and silence us.

Of course, everyone, on whichever side of an argument they sit, is entitled to lawful free speech and to voice their opinion. It is perfectly reasonable, and in fact desirable, to be met with conflicting views. Open debate is how we evolve our thinking. It is also what free and democratic societies are founded upon. However, the last few years have created a culture of bullying, censorship and fear around debate. Dictatorial behaviours were rewarded during the pandemic, with many members of the public fostering a penchant for enforcing rules on others. I feel we each have a duty to oppose this trend before our conversational landscape shrinks to the point that no one feels safe to express a lawful, yet controversial, opinion.

In speaking out, we may also be rebelling against ourselves. Going against our old and outdated modes of behaviour which keep us more or less silent. It will probably feel counter-intuitive to put ourselves at risk of being marginalised and attacked. Even more so to risk potential financial and reputational damage. But something just clicks inside us when we decide that enough is enough. Our stagnant self-censorship and silence feels more damaging than the prospect and consequences of publicly sharing our opinions. Once fully embarked on our free speech quest, these feelings of insecurity and self-doubt come and go. The spirit of rebellion starts to burn in our hearts and our determination and ability to stand our ground grows stronger.

This is also when some of those who have attempted to silence us begin to shy away. Discrimination and harassment against someone for holding a perfectly lawful but different opinion to ourselves is abhorrent. People who behave like that are inherently weak. Which is why many of them retreat when we stand up to them. I have had this experience myself. Some of the most brutal and vocal people who have tried to silence me have suddenly disappeared once I have stood my ground. I have then continued to voice my opinions in a calm but firm manner. In turn, this makes the bullies look unreasonable and irrational, after which they often cease their attacks.

Unless we rebel against the increasing censorship and control around what we say, the boundaries of our free speech will diminish. For example, it has become a taboo to state that only a woman can menstruate or that a man cannot give birth. This goes far beyond the realms of gender identification and deep into the territory of complete delusion. But because the subject is so sensitive, an increasing number of people dare not contradict the fallacy that a biological man can have a period or birth a child. People fear being labelled as a transphobe and a bigot. They know that they could be sanctioned at work and suffer reputational damage if they point out the obvious. However, if none of us are prepared to call out these irrational beliefs, the lies will simply perpetuate. I also feel strongly that a veneer of tolerance and inclusion (both of which I agree with) have been weaponised around this subject and create division and intolerance instead.

So I recommend that we rebel, intelligently, against our own self-censorship and the attempts to silence us from others. Expressing our opinions clearly, calmly and with conviction. Respecting the fact that others will inevitably hold opposing views, debating them, and agreeing to disagree if necessary.

Risk-taking

The safe option, in the short-term, is to remain silent. There is no doubt about that. It is unlikely that anything negative will immediately happen to someone who says nothing. They will be left alone and their lives will continue as normal. In the long run, however, remaining silent could be the least safe option. The future is created, in part, by our actions in the present. For example, allowing dystopian laws and systems to evolve unchecked will mean that they eventually become the norm. On a micro level, allowing an individual in our lives to bully and harass us will not make the situation go away. We might enjoy days or even weeks and months without being attacked, but only until the bully turns on us again. Over time, we then lose confidence, our self-respect diminishes and we may find ourselves in perilous situations. Although it is not an easy thing to do, standing up for ourselves and speaking our mind is better for us in the long-run. This will involve us taking risks.

Voicing controversial opinions will invariably lead to us being attacked, marginalised and encouraged to feel that we are wrong. Speaking our mind could then result in a range of personal losses. We already exist within a culture of fear around lawful free speech. Our social media conversations are monitored and fact-checked. People whisper about vaccines and identity politics, worried that they might be overheard. Those with prominent profiles, who dare to voice unsanctioned opinions, are smeared in the press. Meanwhile, people endorsing the views which we are encouraged to have are celebrated and rewarded for voicing them.

However, in the long-run, the harms resulting from us not speaking out could be far worse. Staying silent about the things which matter now will not improve the situation. The Covid pandemic demonstrated how people will stand back in silence as harms take place around them. Waiting for others to sort out problems or hoping that issues will simply disappear on their own. For example, many people chose not to voice their concerns about lockdowns, despite predicting that they would cause economic ruin and harm the most vulnerable in society. Now those predictions are unfolding catastrophically. As we all know, most people remained silent while children were encouraged to be vaccinated against their parents' wishes, knowing that this was unethical, unscientific and harmful. What else could people turn a blind eye to? How long before the consequences of remaining silent come to their door?

What will they do when there is no one left to fight on their behalf? These are important questions.

Unfortunately, like rebellion, risk-taking is uncomfortable. It is usually difficult and exhausting. It is also potentially rewarding, on a personal level. It can feel exhilarating and empowering. Frightening as well as enlightening. Of course, if it was easy, it would not be risky. Which is why we are told to avoid risk and to seek out safety and certainty instead. A society of risk-takers is hard to control. Unpredictable and dangerous to the status quo. Which is why, when it comes to our free speech, we must embrace risk-taking and use it to our advantage.

Resilience

Speaking out about controversial and sensitive subjects requires resilience. Unfortunately, there is no easy way to cultivate this trait. But then that is the point of it. We build resilience by moving out of our comfort zones. The more we do it, the stronger and more resilient we become. I believe that it is because we have come to expect our lives to be easy and free from struggle that we often avoid moving beyond comfort. We are used to convenience and relative luxury. Most people can simply flick a switch to turn the heating on in their home or to cook some food. Most of us have clean running water, access to the resources we need and not struggling with basic survival.

When it comes to our free speech, we are understandably happier if people are not attacking us for expressing our opinions. It is therefore easier, in the short-term, to stay silent. To remain within our comfort zones and to self-censor. But like all things which require us to expand, standing up and speaking out gets easier the more that we do it. When we begin to express our opinions within potentially hostile environments, the experience is hard at first. There will be attempts to silence us and it will feel uncomfortable. This is also when we have the potential to grow and develop because of the challenge. Moving through the discomfort and overcoming our difficulties will make us stronger.

It is important to be strategic and intuitive when deciding to express our opinions. There is an ebb and a flow to the process. Too much conflict and heat, as a result of expressing our opinions, can risk an early burn out. Equally, fooling ourselves that our silence about controversial topics will make the problem go away is unrealistic. We need to embrace the reality that speaking out will be both hard and rewarding.

Every mythological hero builds their resilience by embarking on their quest. The trials and tribulations of the adventure puts them to the test and hones their skills. Heroes achieving their goals against the odds and realising that they are stronger than they previously thought are found within every quest. So too are the moments when they doubt their abilities and feel that they are losing. Battling against adversity within the outer world and dealing with their inner conflicts is not easy. However, without these elements, they are not on a real quest.

I have written extensively about resilience and the need to foster this trait. My previous books, *"Playing With Fire" "Wild Thing" and "Rewilding Childhood"* all have chapters dedicated to it. At the school where I was the headteacher for twenty years, I developed a whole curriculum for building resilience in children. I taught them on our farmland, in all weathers, and saw how they developed this trait by regularly moving out of their comfort zones. Battling against the elements in the rain or in sub-zero temperatures, even the most fragile of children would grow in strength over time. Resilience cannot be developed conceptually or without hard work. It requires a person to do things which feel uncomfortable and to move through resistance. When they do not succeed, they must get up and do it again.

When it comes to our free speech, resilience is cultivated by speaking our truth in the face of opposition. The more that we do it the stronger we become. Rebellion, risk-taking and resilience go hand in hand. None of them are easy, but all of them combined are practically invincible.

Free speech is dangerous only to those who seek to control the conversational landscape. For each of us, this is an opportunity to step out into a genuine quest. To hone untapped skills and to defend our hard own freedoms as a society. A gift to ourselves, to our children and to the rest of humanity.

Vera Sharav. Holocaust survivor and human rights activist.
Film director of *"Never Again is Now Global"*.

Chapter 4: Imagination in the Battle for Free Speech

"If you fall in love with the imagination, you understand that it is a free spirit. It will go anywhere and it can do anything."

Alice Walker

The importance of being able to speak our truth becomes clear if we imagine living in a world in which expressing an unsanctioned opinion is completely forbidden. For example, not just suppressed, attacked and sanctioned for questioning the government, but far worse. A potential future reality which is entirely possible if we allow a culture of censorship and self-censorship to grow without any resistance. Imagine what the future might look like by following the trajectory of past and current events.

You do not have to look far to find dystopias, steeped

in surveillance, censorship and punishment. They exist where totalitarian regimes rule today. North Korea is a clear example. China, under the Chinese Communist Party, is another. The incarceration and persecution of the Uyghurs is evidence of this. So too is the Chinese Social Credit System. When citizens say or do anything which the authorities dislike, their freedoms are curtailed.

During the Covid pandemic, we witnessed a range of techniques employed by world governments, in partnership with Big Tech and the media, to silence dissenting voices. Alternative views were demonised and attacked and people were warned not to share opinions which questioned the official line. In Canada, during the Truckers Protest against the Covid vaccine mandates, activists and their supporters had their bank accounts frozen by the Canadian government. Post-pandemic de-banking on the grounds of political belief has also happened in the UK and the censorship of alternative views online continues across the globe. The censorship industrial complex is embedded and growing by the day.

During the pandemic era, health professionals, in positions of expertise and able to offer valuable insights, were shut out of crucial debates. Many people, including myself, who questioned the official pandemic response were de-platformed from social media and smeared in the mainstream press. Many medical professionals and others lost their livelihoods and had their reputations damaged as a consequence of voicing their lawful opinions. Individuals within the education sector, journalism, politics, the publishing world and the legal profession were equally vilified and attacked if they expressed "unsanctioned" views.

Along with other professionals who I have campaigned alongside, many of us were also spied on by the UK government for expressing counter-narrative views. The British Military of Defence was directed to carry out these operations in partnership with Big Tech. Subject Access Requests (SARs), which were submitted to various UK Government departments, revealed to many of us that we had been closely monitored. A SAR, which I submitted, revealed that I had been monitored by the UK Government's Counter Disinformation Unit (CDU). This was for expressing my concerns about the Covid vaccine rollout to children. I was then permanently banned from Twitter 1.0, until I was reinstated a year later under Elon Musk.

I was also repeatedly warned by colleagues and authority figures not to speak out or to question any of the pandemic measures. From the potential harms of lockdowns to my views about the Covid vaccines for children, I was constantly told to be silent. Along with many others, I experienced an environment of extreme censorship and then punishment for asking reasonable questions. Chillingly, it was often my colleagues within the education sector who became the most ardent censors. Reporting me to the authorities and calling for investigations into my conduct for voicing my lawful opinions within my own time.

A Dangerous Lack of Imagination

An unimaginative person may read this and conclude that it was an isolated event. They might parrot the conventional viewpoint that the pandemic was an unprecedented situation resulting in unusual but relatively harmless practices. With my own experience of being scrutinised and attacked for expressing my opinions, I have had people tell me that I deserved the treatment which I received. I knew what the rules were and what the punishments might be, so it served me right. However, people with little imagination will not think it possible that their own views and opinions could become the subject of censorship in the future. Or that their religious beliefs and political opinions could be deemed inappropriate by the state at some point. Creeping totalitarianism, as we are witnessing in the Western world, can result in overt dictatorships. Authoritarian regimes defined by the erosion of individual rights, total control over freedom and harsh punishments for dissident voices.

A lack of imagination will lead to the conclusion that whatever the state and mainstream media say must be true. Or at least that the official narrative must be adhered to until we are informed otherwise. I find it bizarre how people can completely change their beliefs and contradict what they have previously thought when instructed to do so. It appears that as long as the message is coming from an organisation or individual in authority, most people will do, say and believe as they are told.

This is one of the reasons why imagination is trivialised within our society, along with playfulness and other traits associated with childhood. An unimaginative population is easy to control and exactly what tyrannical groups and individuals want those they oppress to be. If a person is imaginative, they can creatively work out a way to escape their predicament. They can also use their imagination to project into the unfolding future and see that their compliance will only make matters worse. Not just for them but for their children and for the generations to come.

We have all heard *"playing is a waste of time" "get*

your head out of the clouds" and *"curiosity killed the cat"* along with other untrue and unhelpful statements. In reality, the opposite is true. We should all spend time imagining different scenarios, being curious and asking questions, playing with ideas and engaging our creativity.

Playground Bullies

One of the ways in which people are bullied into silence is through the use of name calling. During the pandemic, we were told by politicians and mainstream media that national lockdowns were necessary and beneficial to society. We were later told by many of the same politicians and media pundits that lockdowns had caused immeasurable harm. However, those who dared to point out the obvious economic and societal consequences of lockdowns at the time were often labelled as conspiracy theorists. We were accused of being far-right extremists and by default that meant that we must be racist and bigoted. The accusation of racism, including anti-Semitism, has been weaponised against many dissident voices, even when they are anything but that. The reason for this is that racism and anti-Semitism are abhorrent and most people, hopefully, are against discrimination of this kind. However, an unimaginative person reading the news headlines is unlikely to do their own research and to think critically about these slurs.

The accusations will be taken on face value and without question. So the dissident voices become discredited and marginalised. This is one of the reasons why so many people kept their views to themselves during the pandemic, even if they disagreed with what was happening. No one likes to be called names or to be accused of things which are untrue. It creates negative feelings, damages reputations and takes a great deal of energy to respond to. People with limited imagination and a diminished critical thinking capacity will believe what they are told. Even when their previous knowledge and experience of people they know has painted a completely different picture.

I liken the behaviour of the authorities and media to that of playground bullies. Having taught children in schools for thirty years, I have come across a minority who are bullies. They use name calling as one of their primary tools of assault. Making up stories about others is another common behaviour. They aim to marginalise and to punish those they wish to oppress. Bullies, whether adult or child, are also very weak and secretly under-confident. In some cases they might possess physical strength and social status, but they are always disempowered and desperately scared on the inside. This is without exception. Happy, contented and empowered individuals never bully others. They draw strength from within rather than insatiably taking energy from other people. I have also noticed that playground bullies are invariably unimaginative and scathing of those whose imagination abounds. Again, a comparison can be made here with totalitarians. They fear our imagination and can only deal with it by trying to suppress it. Belittling us when we present our concerns about the future and declaring that our thoughts are just paranoid conspiracies.

Imagination and the Heroic Quest

Stepping out into the quest requires courage. Speaking our truth in an age of lies is not easy and it is likely that we will be attacked for it. However, every reluctant hero eventually knows in their heart that it is down to them to attain the goal of their quest. Something which they do, not just for themselves, but for humanity at large. The hero is able to imagine what their world could be like if they continue to reject their call to adventure. Eventually realising that they must embark on their quest, despite their understandable fears and uncertainty about it. As they step out into the journey, their imagination is used to predict and problem solve as they make their way. The success of their quest is dependent on them utilising their imagination and creativity. Predicting the next move by their foes and working out what can be done to outwit them. Odysseus engages his creativity and imagination throughout his adventures. Outwitting his foes with unexpected twists and turns and winning the admiration of the Greek gods with his ideas. He also becomes the focus of attacks due to his unwillingness to give up. Heroes are admired by the strong and envied by the weak.

I believe that for each of us our imagination is our superpower. Which is why it is vilified and challenged by authoritarians. If we can imagine a way out of tyranny, it can act as a guiding light and glimmer of hope for each of us. Escaping from an abusive relationship, such as a violent partnership, a bullying employer or an authoritarian state, requires us to use our imagination. Then, once we have embarked on our journey, we need to imagine our way through it. Thinking creatively about the different routes we might take while continuously visualising the future life of freedom we desire.

We also need to engage our imaginations when summoning our inner hero. When we read about the great heroic quests in ancient mythology, watch a hero in a film or witness one in real life, we feel inspired. It is not uncommon for us to imagine what it would be like if we were a hero too. Perhaps indulging in a daydream in which we are heroic and triumphing over adversity. We start to feel a brimming excitement inside us at this point. A sense of determination and empowerment. Our feelings often then translate into our body language. Head held high, straight back and chest open. We experience a myriad of physical and emotional responses when we invoke our inner hero in this way.

For many people, this fleeting experience is often followed by self-doubt and negative messaging, *"I'm not really a hero", "I haven't got what it takes", "I don't have special powers or gifts"*. All of which are untrue. We have already looked at our resistance to the quest and how almost every hero is, at first, reluctant to embark on their journey. We have also examined the ways in which we try to avoid life's challenges and how every hero feels self-doubt and despair at points throughout their adventure. This is all part of the quest. Without the resistance, we are not on a quest at all. The experience has to feel challenging and able to move us beyond our comfort zones. Discovery of new powers and skills, which the hero had not previously used, is also part of every quest. Including the realisation that they already possess various traits which were previously dormant.

Again, this is arguably the purpose of any heroic quest. The end goal and journey itself are means by which the individual gains insight into who they really are. Only by taking a leap of faith, entering the quest and facing its many challenges, can we discover what we are truly made of. No wonder the archetype of the hero is steadily being eroded and replaced with helpless alternatives within popular culture. The last thing totalitarians want is to be pitched against heroes. Empowered individuals who are resilient, imaginative, rebellious and willing to take risks. Bullies always back down eventually when confronted by people with these traits. They know that they will lose in the final round.

Imagination is our superpower. There is no doubt about it. It is how we project our minds into future scenarios and problem solve our way out of every trap. Imagination allows us to imagine being a hero and then become one in reality. Feeling the excitement of the quest before we have even embarked on it and visualising our success at the end of our journey. Imagination inspires our critical thinking and our enquiring minds. It is why we are able to question irrational rules and diktats and present alternative proposals. Imagination is limitless.

When it comes to our free speech, imagination is perhaps our greatest ally. Finding new and creative ways to express our views. Articulating imagined future realities, when we have followed a clear trajectory based on past and current events. Imagination allows us to exercise our right to free speech with the feeling and stance of a hero. When we engage our imagination, we discover powerful character traits and skills which can be used creatively to improve our own lives and those of others.

The role of imagination in the fight for free speech cannot be overstated. Every revolution started in someone's mind. Imagining the future they desired for themselves and for their children, then imagining how to achieve that end. We must stop allowing the authoritarians to silence us into submission. They are little more than playground bullies. Begin to stand up to them and express our opinions with confidence and they will soon back down.

Julian Assange. Whistleblower and Founder of WikiLeaks.
Incarcerated since 2019 in HM Belmarsh Prison.

Chapter 5: Cultivating Optimism and Gratitude on the Quest

*"We are the ones we've
been waiting for"*

Hopi Indian Elders

S tanding up for our right to free speech with a feeling of defeat and negativity could jeopardise what we wish to achieve. Many of us complain about the erosion of free speech, censorship and other people's silence on important topics, but how much does that improve matters? Complaining definitely raises awareness of the problem, which is the first step to sorting it out. Without awareness nothing can be done. Pointing out what is wrong may also rally likeminded individuals and groups around a common cause or campaign. But negative thoughts and statements only go so far in resolving the issue. Being more optimistic about the future and the outcome of our battles can move us closer to our desired goals. Cultivating a sense of gratitude for what is going well, while remaining focussed during the fight, can be greatly beneficial.

Optimism

As difficult as it may be to summon at times, a glimmer of optimism can support us in achieving the future we wish to see. Shining a light during times of darkness and illuminating our path ahead. The free speech landscape is continuously narrowing under new laws, online censorship and societal changes. The trajectory of which leads us to a potential future steeped in sanctions for simply expressing what we believe. A world of social credit systems, de-banking for voicing our opinions, being outcast from our groups and having our freedoms curtailed. As bleak and depressing as this future dystopia sounds, pointing out the real danger of it manifesting is necessary. Many people have no idea that we are moving in this direction as a society, and therefore have no concerns whatsoever. However, focussing our attention on the problem must be balanced with actively creating a range of positive solutions. In order for us to bring about these solutions we will require at least a dash of optimism. Cultivating a belief that our efforts to defend our hard won civic freedoms will eventually bear fruit. Knowing, on an intuitive level, that we are going to win and visualising with absolute clarity the future we each wish to see.

There are excellent reasons why a more optimistic outlook on life is better than a pessimistic one. If we adopt a pessimistic attitude, and enter the realm of depression, we can easily jeopardise our health. Our immune system can weaken and levels of cortisol and other stress hormones begin to rise within us. Stress hormones attack white blood cells, which are a crucial part of our immune response. When cortisol levels increase, our ability to respond effectively to infectious diseases decreases, and our ability to fight various cancers is reduced. Optimism, on the other hand, creates a buffer against the probability of experiencing depression. Not only does optimism reduce stress, it also increases dopamine levels. Dopamine is a neurotransmitter that makes us feel happy, motivated and more confident to take risks. Optimistic people are happier, have more productive relationships and they cope better in challenging situations.

Within the context of our free speech, and expressing controversial or politically sensitive opinions, optimism can be a powerful ally. Staying focussed on our goals, and feeling confident that we will attain them, will help us navigate our way through our quest. Particularly during times when we are attacked by others for voicing our opinions.

Gratitude

As a free speech advocate, and having been attacked for being one, I have found myself slipping into pessimism at times. Reputational damage, harm to my livelihood, smears in the press and the other negative consequences of speaking my mind, occasionally take their toll. Many of us who have publicly commented on controversial topics have been attacked and subsequently incurred losses. When this happens, our survival instinct kicks in. We wonder how we will overcome our challenges, how we will pay our bills and meet our family commitments. Things which we may have previously taken for granted without much worry. Our urgent need for survival can then lead to desperate thoughts and actions. I am not immune to this myself and is one of the reasons why I have written *The Hero's Voice*. I would like my experience of having my free speech attacked to be of value to others. Being honest about how difficult it can be, but also how empowering and enlightening it ultimately is.

Author and professor of psychology, Dr. Robert Emmons, is regarded as the world's leading expert on gratitude. His research has revealed that expressing heartfelt thanks improves our feelings of self-esteem. His research also shows less obvious outcomes. For example, expressing gratitude can lead to a strengthened heart, a more robust immune system and decreased blood pressure. Dr. Emmons' research also demonstrates that our academic intelligence expands and our capacity for forgiveness increases when we say what we are thankful for.

Personally, I find that I feel immediately uplifted, lighter and more relaxed when I have listed the things for which I am grateful. My negative self-talk recedes and I appreciate the things which are going well in my life. Making the effort to be thankful for what is going well has helped me enormously during my free speech battle. This has then enabled me to become more optimistic and therefore work out a way to overcome my various challenges. My sense of gratitude has also inspired me to never give up

A Light in the Darkness

"If we realise that we live in a powerful world full of energy, and that energy is a creative energy of the universe, and our power is the spiritual power of aligning ourselves, then we are very powerful"

Vandana Shiva

Going against the grain and voicing our opinions about controversial and politically sensitive subjects can get very dark at times. It invites what seems like relentless attacks and smears. Our lives may become extremely challenging if we get marginalised by our friends, family and colleagues. We may worry about our finances and work opportunities and wonder how we will cope. These are all valid concerns and inevitable consequences if we are in a minority of people expressing controversial opinions. In my case, because I was the only headteacher or school principal to voice my concerns about lockdowns, masking kids and the vaccine rollout to children, I was easy pickings for those who disagreed with my views. I then incurred a range of hardships, including all of those listed above and more. But going very deeply within myself to find optimism, and listing the many things for which I feel grateful, has helped enormously. This has then inspired another journey, which Vandana Shiva captures so well in her quote. A spiritual dimension to the free speech quest and discovery of my own *Hero's Voice*. The feeling that I am on the side of light and love in this great battle against darkness. Making connections with likeminded individuals and opening myself to helpful synchronicities along the way. I believe that this is another core purpose of a true quest? To align ourselves with the divine and to find answers to our spiritual questions. Eventually creating the future of freedom we wish to see for us and our children.

Fostering a sense of optimism and gratitude opens doors which are hard to find when we feel pessimistic and defeated. These positive traits can be cultivated while on our quest and pave the way for the outcome we desire.

The Great Awakening

Many of us have been raised to believe that our biggest problems can only be solved with the help of a group or individual other than ourselves. Our saviours come in many different guises. It might be through the acquisition of marketed products, the promises of a political party at election time, or our perception of an individual who we hope is able to solve our problems. However, our true point of power lies within each of us. We have the ability to overcome life's challenges from where we are right now. But we must trust our instincts and listen to our intuition in order to do this. We must ultimately see ourselves as powerful instead of helpless. This is in contrast to how the authorities want us to view ourselves.

Again, we are invited to rebel against the disempowering message that we do not already possess the skills and strengths to survive and thrive. It is why during the pandemic we were told not to trust our gut and intuitive feelings. We were also instructed not to think or to question things. Our thoughts and feelings were wrong and potentially dangerous, so we were encouraged to pass our decision making over to the authorities.

Our fear based modern culture, within which we are told to fear uncertainty in order to avert disaster, is illogical. This approach does not shield us from life's knocks and losses at all. No amount of cotton wool will protect us from the inevitability of death, for example. When those who we have been encouraged to trust in authority turn out to be untrustworthy, we are provided with excuses for their behaviour. Never are we advised to trust our own judgements and instincts instead. This is neither healthy nor sustainable.

As previously mentioned, at the start of almost every mythological quest, the hero feels self-doubt and lacks confidence. *"Why have you chosen me? I'm the wrong person for this quest"* they say. Stumbling and falling as they advance along their adventure. But as time passes by, they learn how to cope. They become more resilient and sharpen their instincts. On their journey, the great heroes of mythology begin to develop an acute sense of intuition and inner wisdom which is forged by the adventure itself. This is exactly why tyrannical authorities want us to play it safe and to stay within the sanctuary of the known. They are fully aware that stepping out into our individual quests is how we become self-empowered and therefore less easy to control.

The process, as mentioned before, is driven by "nostos". The sense of wanting to return home, to a sense of completion and fulfilment. Self-censoring out of fear of reprisals can never navigate us to that place. We can only ever feel incomplete by continuing in that manner, with a simmering fear of what others may do and say to us.

Every once in a while, there is a collective response to societal conditions which causes people to awaken. These are times when people will talk about the end of the world and the beginning of a new one. I believe that we are in such a time now. A great awakening involving individuals and communities who are re-evaluating their needs and priorities. This often happens when we face adversity in our personal lives and then reconsider what is important to us. It can also happen on a mass scale after traumatic events such as wars, economic crises and other societal changes. Governments which have often been complicit in the trauma then rush to provide solutions. A mass awakening starts to emerge when the people no longer believe in the solutions being offered to them. They see through the promises and platitudes and want to create their own solutions instead. At a macro scale, this is the hero's journey at a population level. It is clear that we are in a time like that now. More people are waking up than ever before and the prospect of positive change feels inevitable. Again, a sense of optimism and gratitude are essential here. We will not create a future of freedom from a place of fear and pessimism.

Our free speech is pivotal to this transformative time. On an individual level as well as a societal one. This is our invitation to change the course of history and create the world of opportunity and freedom that we all wish to see. However, it can only come about if we are willing to answer our individual call to the quest with affirmative action. To embark on our epic journey, despite our fears, and to meet the challenge head on. Remaining within the confines and safety of the known is a temporary illusion. Eventually, the problem will come to our door, by which time it might be too late to fight back. It could be our individual religious or political beliefs which come under fire next time or some other fundamental core value which is stripped away from us. Do not let that happen. Stand up and speak out about the things which matter. When we accept the call to the quest, and use our hero's voice, we will be victorious.

Anita McKone and Robert Burrows. Founders of
the worldwide non-violent resistance movement
"We Are Human We Are Free"

Chapter 6: The Homecoming

"To travel home and see the dawn. And if a god will wreck me yet again on the wine-dark sea, I can bear that too, with a spirit tempered to endure, bring the trial on!"

Odysseus

B efore the Covid pandemic, I was regarded as the golden boy of my profession and could do no wrong. Running a large school of 365 pupils and managing sixty members of staff, I was acclaimed for my innovations within the education sector. Alongside the usual lessons you would expect to find in a school, I created an engaging rural curriculum for the children in my care. I ran a school farm on 120 acres of marshland opposite the school site and taught my children farming and survival skills. On this land, I also taught my pupils to safely shoot 410 bore shotguns, skin rabbits, pluck pigeons, and to light and cook over an open fire. You would be forgiven for thinking that this might have led to complaints, but this did not happen. Instead, I was congratulated and supported by the authorities and by the general public for my approach to education. I enjoyed widespread positive media coverage and had an excellent reputation. Of course, this all changed when I spoke out about the UK government's response to Covid and its impact on children. Particularly when I expressed my concerns about the Covid vaccine rollout to children.

My opinion regarding the Covid vaccines for children has always been that we should not give a child a medical intervention unless there is a clear benefit and a proven safety record. It is important to remember that before 2020 it would have been extreme to have argued otherwise. I have always repeated the same key points when voicing my concerns.

1. Children are at extremely low risk of serious illness from Covid.

2. The Covid vaccines pose known risks and have no long-term safety data.

3. A child can still catch and spread Covid when vaccinated against the virus.

4. In my personal opinion the risks from the Covid

vaccines outweigh any possible benefit for a child.

Despite the above amounting to lawful free speech and being factually accurate, it was enough to trigger some people to attack me for expressing these views. I now know why that is.

There is a vast censorship industrial complex being created across the globe. It is designed to silence dissenting voices. Those who dare to question the official narrative on a wide and evolving range of topics. As I experienced myself, dissidents are often framed as dangerous extremists. This is one of the ways in which the authorities attempt to scare off others who are considering speaking out.

I was anonymously reported to my former employer and investigated on three separate occasions. On the last occasion, I was also reported to the Department for Education's Counter Extremism Division and reported under the UK Government's Counter Terrorism policy. My alleged offence was to have publicly raised concerns about lockdowns, masking and the Covid vaccine rollout to children. Opinions which I had expressed in my own time and in a lawful and respectful manner. Three independent investigations concluded that I had done nothing wrong and the complaints were later dropped. I was also cleared by the Counter Extremism Division. They could see very clearly that I had acted within the law and spoken moderately about my valid concerns. However, it seemed very strange to me at the time that the expression of my free speech could lead to such a dramatic response.

Within the UK, there are a number of factors which created the conditions for this series of events to take place. During the pandemic, the government set up a psychological Nudge Unit which was designed to influence public opinion. They used fear tactics and coercion to make people disproportionately scared of Covid and compliant with the various draconian measures they introduced. The use of a Counter Disinformation Unit (CDU) was also employed. The CDU monitored the social media activity of anyone who questioned the government's Covid response. I was monitored and subsequently banned from Twitter 1.0, as well as suspended from other platforms because of this organisation. The CDU had previously been used to monitor foreign adversaries prior to the Covid pandemic but was repurposed to spy on the domestic population during the pandemic. Furthermore, the British intelligence agencies, such as MI5 and MI6, liaised with the CDU to monitor and stifle public debate about the official pandemic response. The British Military of Defence (MoD) was also watching and recording the online activity of members of the public. The now infamous 77th Brigade, a unit of the

British Army, was charged with identifying and reporting those who questioned government policy on Covid. Again, this unit had previously been used to track down terrorists and foreign adversaries.

The tactics used by the Nudge Unit were highly effective in rallying support from the general public. They were able to encourage many people to do things which they did not authentically believe in and to stay quiet about it. This included speaking up about the inevitable harms caused by lookdowns and the Covid vaccine rollout to children. Within the UK, almost 90% of parents of five to eleven year olds declined to accept the offer of giving the vaccine to their children. This is despite a multi-million pound advertising campaign designed to persuade and coerce them into doing so. This means that the vast majority of parents presumably weighed up the risks and benefits and decided against their children receiving the Covid vaccine. However, hardly anyone spoke up about it at the time and those who did were publicly vilified. My headteacher and school principal colleagues also chose to remain silent. Many of them told me privately that they had serious concerns but that they feared the consequences of publicly expressing their views.

Now that I know that I was monitored by the likes of the CDU, and that the pandemic was set within the backdrop of the censorship industrial complex, it is clear why events unfolded in the way that they did. Members of the public were encouraged to hound out dissenting voices or to self-censor if they agreed with them.

People who had been evangelised by the now debunked "Safe and Effective" mantra set about hunting down those who questioned government policy on Covid. This is what I have described as "Britain's unofficial social credit system". In other words, seeking to punish dissenting voices via the complaints process and cancel culture.

The attacks on my lawful free speech eventually compelled me to take my employer to court. Something which is ongoing and which I have one of the best legal teams in the land backing me. My barrister, Paul Diamond, is the UK's leading civil liberties barrister. He is frequently cited by notable judges and referenced on almost every law degree course in Britain. I have also gained the support of elements of the UK's mainstream media, such and The Telegraph and high-profile journalists, including Molly Kingsley and Allison Pearson. Through the darkness I have managed to find companions who share the same passion for free speech as I do. Lawyers, media pundits, Members of Parliament and medical professionals. A small but growing band of freedom fighters at the top of their respective fields of expertise.

I began writing *The Hero's Voice* when I was feeling lost at the start of this journey. I wanted to discover ways to inspire others to speak out as well as find answers to my own questions about this process. In doing so, I discovered my own inner gifts and insights which I have shared within the pages of this book. Ultimately, my own free speech quest has liberated me. I have found my inner light and feel stronger and more confident than ever before. Ironically, the attempts to silence me have had the opposite effect. I now have a bigger platform and wider reach than at any previous point in my life.

Within the mythological quest, the central character is resistant at first. They then weigh up the costs of declining the call to the quest with the possible outcome of accepting it. They always conclude that remaining within the relative comfort of their current life will only delay the inevitable conflict of the quest. Once on their journey, the hero continues to feel self-doubt at times and wonders whether they will achieve their goal. Simultaneously, through the act of moving beyond their comfort zone, they grow stronger and more resilient. As the quest progresses, they often meet allies and mentors and discover inner, sometimes magical, gifts. Eventually they return home, stronger and wiser than before, and in the full knowledge of their potential and true purpose in life.

This is the opportunity presented by *The Hero's Voice* and our individual call to the quest. To use the public expression of our opinions as a vehicle for self-discovery and to take an active role in the global battle for free speech. Our homecoming, towards the future of freedom we each desire, is our Odyssey. An opportunity to be triumphant at this turning point in history and forge our own mythological story to inspire the generations to come. Self-censoring out of fear of reprisals will not win the day. Only becoming the hero we were all sent here to be will do that. It is time to pick up our swords and shields and to step into the quest.

John Lennon. Lead singer of The Beatles and political activist.

Also by Mike Fairclough

Playing with Fire
Embracing risk and danger in schools

Wild Thing
Embracing Childhood Traits in Adulthood
for a Happier, More Carefree Life

Rewilding Childhood
Raising Resilient Children Who Are
Adventurous, Imaginative and Free